# Therefore I Am

# Therefore I Am

## A Book for African-American Men

*Frederick B. Covington*

iUniverse, Inc.
New York  Lincoln  Shanghai

# Therefore I Am
## A Book for African-American Men

iUniverse books may be ordered through booksellers or by contacting:

iUniverse
2021 Pine Lake Road, Suite 100
Lincoln, NE 68512
www.iuniverse.com
1-800-Authors (1-800-288-4677)

ISBN: 0-595-34283-3

Printed in the United States of America

# Contents

# *Introduction*

Throughout history, African-American men have persevered through trial after trial. Being subject to practices such as segregation and publicly acceptable discrimination has shackled our progress in the past, and situations such as socioeconomic disadvantage, stereotyping, ongoing indirect discrimination, and other situations and practices continue to hinder us today.

Through it all we have walked out of and through the wreckage of unfairness and have faced a world that has on several occasions treated us unjustly. This we continue to do on a daily basis.

*Therefore I Am* takes a look at the quotes, parables, idioms, and other sayings that have kept African-American men focused and headed in the right direction. We look at the sayings that have guided African-American men down the path of righteousness and respect, even though we are frequently faced with easier means and opportunities that would detour us from this just path along life's journey. In a world where the athlete makes $30 million a year and the teacher makes $30,000 a year, it becomes more and more of a challenge to remain just in a society that at times seems to have a skewed sense of values.

Nevertheless, this is the world in which we live. We must continue to push forward. We are a people who persevere and strive not to let the missteps or misfortunes of our past cause us to stumble in our futures. Within this text are the thoughts and experiences of everyday African-American men, those you see on a daily basis—no extraordinary tales of fame and fortune—but instead *successes* in the truest sense of the word.

These are our thoughts; these are our perceptions.

—Frederick B. Covington

# Intelligence

## "An intelligent man would never resort to profanity to speak his mind."

Enlightenment:
Being a man of color, there are so many ways and situations this quote has helped me endure. Through this quote I have come to realize that a man curses because he does not know the correct words to use to properly relate his thoughts or feelings. A man's use and choice of words is a direct reflection of his inner being and character. How many times have you heard Michael Jordan, Bill Cosby, Will Smith, Ali, Malcolm X, Martin Luther King, or any truly intelligent black man use profanity? Take your time and think of those you know who do use profanity, and compare them to those who don't. I am most certain that those who don't, you will find, have more positive things going on for themselves than the others. The quote has always guided me. This is in all circumstances—school, work, home, and so on.

It has aided me in my daily living by helping me maintain the image I always wish to present: a clean one, a positive one, and an intelligent one.

### Therefore I Am
*Age*: 50
*Occupation*:
Managerial Professional
*City, State*:
Yazoo City, MS
*Interests and Organizations*:
I am a father, civil war enthusiast, military historian, avid reader, church youth ministry leader, Prince-Hall Shriner, Alpha Phi Alpha

> ## "There is only one thing more painful than learning from experience, and that is not learning from experience."

Enlightenment:
Throughout our lives we make one mistake after another. These mistakes should serve as points of growth and development for us to better ourselves. What's sad is that some people come out of hard and difficult situations without a single lesson learned. They are destined to repeat the same mistakes over and over again. The person who doesn't learn from mistakes is foreshadowing a life of stagnancy. For all situations you go through that don't go exactly the way you want—analyze them. Search out the mistake and learn from your prior actions. Ask yourself who, what, when, why, and where. This will improve your outlook because you will realize exactly where you went wrong, and you will not relive defeat time and time again.

### Therefore I Am
Age: 27
Occupation:
High School Teacher
City, State:
Charlotte, North Carolina
Interests and Organizations:
Auto mechanics, NAACP Chapter President

> ## "An error does not become a mistake until you choose to ignore it."

**Enlightenment:**

This was told to me by my father. It has taught me that I need to be thorough in everything that I do throughout life, and to realize when there is a wrong in my life—whether it is mental, physical, or even a relationship. Moreover, it has taught me to quickly readjust or fix the circumstances if I feel they are incorrect.

### Therefore I Am

*Age:* 23

*Occupation:*
Graduate Student

*City, State:*
Little Rock, Arkansas

*Interests and Organizations:*
National Honor Society Member, Golf, Soccer, Basketball, Music

## "Being right is highly overrated. Even a stopped clock is right twice a day"

Enlightenment:

This is a quote that you have to look at from different perspectives. First you have to look at it concerning yourself. Don't be boastful whenever you are right about something; this can cause you to loose friends, gain enemies, and just seem obnoxious. On the other hand, when you come across somebody that always claims to be right or knowledgeable, they usually tend to know less than you do. And just because a man or woman is right about one thing, doesn't make him or her an authority on the issue.

### Therefore I Am

*Age:* 52

*Occupation:*

High School Physics Teacher

*City, State:*

Roanoke, Virginia

*Interests and Organizations:*

Teaching in all its various forms to anyone and everyone who wants to learn.

> ## "Life is 10% what happens to you, but 90% on how you deal with it."

Enlightenment:
This saying has kept me out of dozens of negative situations in my life. This saying also reminds me that God gave every man free will, meaning we can choose what we do and what we say, as well as choose what we don't do and what we don't say. Everything has a consequence to it—whether good or bad—it's just taking the time to make the right choice to avoid the bad ones.

## Therefore I Am
*Age:* 25
*Occupation:*
Software Service Technician
*City, State:*
Rock Hill, South Carolina
*Interests and Organizations:*
Enjoy writing songs, reading, spending time with family and friends, listening to music, and being creative. I am a member of Phi Beta Sigma Fraternity, Inc.
Winthrop University Alumni

---

## "Deliberate often, decide once."

Enlightenment:

There are so many choices in life that we have to make—from life-changing choices to the mundane. I have learned that when making these decisions, once you have decided upon a definite, stick with it. Many times, the first decision is the right decision. However, it is of the utmost importance to think of all of your options and any negative repercussions before jumping to any conclusions.

To deliberate means to think about or discuss issues and decisions carefully. Most importantly, always remember that your actions affect others. Always ask yourself the following: How will this decision benefit/hinder me? How will this decision affect my future? How will this decision affect my loved ones?

---

### Therefore I Am

*Age:* 38

*Occupation:*
Inbound Technology/Computer Sales Associate

*City, State:*
Memphis, Tennessee

*Interests and Organizations:*
Omega Psi Phi fraternity, Inc.
Staying involved in my community and working on community beautification projects.

> ## "Never argue with a stupid person.
> ## First they'll drag you down to their level and then
> ## beat you with experience."

Enlightenment:

Having worked in management for several years I've been involved in several disagreements and personal discrepancies. There are some people who will sit down and explain their point of view in a rational manner, but for every one of these personalities, you will have three people who are totally opposite. These are the people who will talk over you while you are talking, interrupt you mid-sentence, or just speak in a louder voice than you.

When an argument becomes a yelling match, the person with the correct point or who is right does not necessarily "win" the argument. It is usually the person who is acting out of control or frantic because he or she always has to have the last word, and usually does. So when you find yourself in a situation or argument with a "stupid" person, let them know that you will continue the discussion after he or she uses the appropriate tone, manner, and respect that you are showing him or her. Let the individual know that the conversation will not resume until he or she does so. Not only will this give you the floor to speak, but you now have the opportunity to express yourself to a party who is more attentive.

### Therefore I Am
Age: 41
Occupation:
Healthcare Account Manager
City, State:
Montgomery, Alabama
Interests and Organizations:
NAACP, Black Panther, Minority Male Consortium

> ## "The young man knows the rules; the old man knows the exceptions."

Enlightenment:
Education can open the doors to many things, such as prosperity, economic uplift, and even change in social status. Though education can bring these things, all the education in the world cannot account for experience and wisdom. I have learned more from my elders than any book or professor can ever teach me. And though I have multiple letters behind my name—PhD, MA, BA—all of my book knowledge cannot hold a candle against what I have learned by just sitting and listening to the lives and experiences of my elders. This is the knowledge that we need to pass down to our children.

### Therefore I Am

*Age:* 45
*Occupation:*
Stock Broker
*City, State:*
Manhattan, New York
*Interests and Organizations:*
Various investment clubs throughout the New York metropolitan area, Big Brothers of NY

> ## "A mind stretched to a new idea never goes back to its original dimensions."

Enlightenment:

Young men, open your minds. Don't get caught up in the status quo. Just because you are a young black male does not mean you have to listen to hip-hop or wear your jeans hanging off your butt. To become a true individual, you must buck trends and be your own person. If you like country and western music, you have the right to explore and enjoy country and western music. It is this stretching of our minds that makes us new thinkers and creators. We must exist outside the box that others have made for us. This is my personal testimony based on my move from a Black community, where the majority of my peers looked, acted, and talked like me, to middle America, where I would be lucky to see one face that looked like mine the entire day. The point I am trying to make is that you can still be a strongly Afrocentric man and have independent thought and actions. Not only was my mind stretched upon my move, but also—for those individuals who got to know the African-American experience through watching *Good Times*, *The Jeffersons*, *Different Strokes*, and other stereotypical shows—their minds were stretched as well when they a met a character who could not be placed on those shows.

## Therefore I Am
*Age:* 30
*Occupation:*
McDonald's Franchise Co-Owner
*City, State:*
Lansing, Michigan
*Interests and Organizations:*
Community outreach programs, Welfare-to-work programs

> ## "A wise man sees as much as he should, not as much as he can."

Enlightenment:

I used to watch a television show when I was a little boy and the character on the show would say, "Just the facts." This, along with the quote above has kept me ahead. I find out what I need to know to better myself and I proceed. I do not linger to watch to see what is going to happen next. This can amount to valuable time lost, which can never be recovered. Case in point: my friends and I would always walk to the basketball court to shoot hoops after school. On the way to the courts, the short way, there was this ferocious dog that terrified the neighborhood. Now, though I knew the dog would always be in its doghouse on the hot afternoons that we would go and play ball, I knew that there was a chance that the dog would chase us down the street once it heard the commotion we made as we approached the house at which it stayed. That's all I needed to know. No point in sticking my hand in the fire to see if it is hot; I already know it is hot! The equation I had in my head was this: *Me + Big No Leashed Dog = Me with a Dog Bite.*

Of course, this did not sit well with me so I found another route; though longer, it was safer. This can apply to all facets of life, so all you really need to know are "just the facts."

## Therefore I Am
*Age:* 34
*Occupation:*
Aeronautical Engineer
*City, State:*
Houston, Texas
*Interests and Organizations:*
Church Choir Director, Organist

> ## "A wise person has something to say; a fool has to say something."

**Enlightenment:**

Shut Up! Shut Up! Shut Up! This is what needs to be said to a lot of brothers all over the world. Some may think harsh of me by saying this, but that still does not change the fact that it needs to be said. Sometimes having to say something only confirms your ignorance and stupidity. For instance, if you are in or around a conversation with auto mechanics who are talking about transmissions, alternators, or engines and you are a doctor, shut up and listen! Though you are a learned man in probably many facets, you do not know everything. Since we are not blessed with omnipotent knowledge, sometimes we need to open our ears and close our mouths.

## Therefore I Am

*Age:* 49

*Occupation:*

Motivational Speaker

*City, State:*

Los Angeles, California

*Interests and Organizations:*

Full-Time father to three wonderful sons

---

## "Every closed eye is not sleeping; and every open eye is not seeing."

Enlightenment:

In life, many things are not what they seem. One must pay very close attention to one's surroundings to truly know what is going on. What you may perceive to be one way may be completely the opposite. My father explained this to me because he was a very meticulous businessman, who paid attention to detail. He spoke of prior business deals that he saw transpire with outside colleagues where with the right hand they will be shaking your hand, and with the left, planting a knife in your back. Always look and see what is behind the smile; it may surprise you. Now that I am older, I apply this quote even to bills and laws passed in the House and the Senate. Look deeply at how these laws "help" us. For instance, consider the Three Strikes and You're Out law, or consider the time one has to spend in prison for the type of drug one is carrying. The least-expensive drugs, which are more obtainable by people of lower socioeconomic status (poorer) are punishable by longer incarceration times than drugs (that are even more potent) used by those who are affluent. Hmmmm....

Wake up brothers—not everything is what it appears to be.

---

## Therefore I Am

*Age:* 38
*Occupation:*
Barber
*City, State:*
Oakland, California
*Interests and Organizations:*
Refurbishing classic cars.

## "Knowledge is power."

Enlightenment:
This is the quote of all quotes, the alpha and the omega. I can find no other statement that holds so true. What you don't know can hurt you. While attending college, my older brother would come home on the weekend and talk about all the exciting times he had experienced the preceding week. Though we would sit and talk for hours, before he left he would always say, "Knowledge is power." He explained it like this:

If you don't know your place, you can be cast aside or ignored.
If you don't know your value, you can be devalued.
If you don't know your rights, you can be treated unjustly.

He would also say that knowledge is something you can attain that no one can take from you; knowledge is your best friend and always will be your most powerful ally in any battle—whatever it may be.

This quote has kept me focused and on the right path since I first heard the words.

## Therefore I Am
*Age:* 26
*Occupation:*
Graduate Student
*City, State:*
Washington, DC
*Interests and Organizations:*
Academic excellence is my only interest at this point in my life.

> ## "The greatest obstacle to discovery is not ignorance—it is the illusion of knowledge."

Enlightenment:
There is nothing sadder than someone who thinks they know what they are talking about and will not listen to anyone else. These people will argue against the preacher over a sermon that he wrote. When someone has in their mind that "I am right" or "I know what I am talking about," their mental gates are closed. They believe that words and information can flow in only one direction: outward. Their minds' inlets are blocked by their illusions of knowledge.

This quote taught me to never close my eyes or ears to anything. Something can be learned from every person you meet.

## Therefore I Am
Age: 63
Occupation:
Proofreader
City, State:
Brooklyn, New York
Interests and Organizations:
Avid reader (comes along with the job)

## "No matter how full the river, it still wants to grow."

Enlightenment:

What I find in our community in many circumstances is complacency. Settling is something that we do far too often. I have seen that this in the case of education, in the workforce, and in life overall. Though a river is full, it still wants to be bigger and more powerful. A river that is now considered "rapids" was once a smooth-flowing stream or brook. We have to liken ourselves to rivers. We have to continue to grow, not settle. One can never grow if he does not get out of his zone of comfort. A little hard work has never harmed anyone.

My grandmother told me this quote when I was a young boy. She would speak of how they used to go to the river and catch fish. She would always tell me that a man's mind and heart should be like a river, always willing to expand and be stretched to new bounds.

### Therefore I Am

*Age:* 64

*Occupation:*
Chief Legal Council

*City, State:*
Luverne, Alabama

*Interests and Organizations:*
City Council Member, Education Board Member, Teacher

# Responsibility

## "To whom much is given, much is required."

Enlightenment:

This is a very simple, yet profound statement. I was told as a young child that opportunities are gifts from God and that we should take advantage of each and every one of them. However, as African-American men, we also have an obligation to give back once we have seized and taken advantage of these opportunities. Because success is predicated on a combination of hard work and luck, we owe it to our ancestors, women, children, and all African peoples to act as Trojan horses.... We should serve as catalysts for change in order to empower others and secure the perpetuation of black progress.

## Therefore I Am

*Age:* 22

*Occupation:*

Student

*City, State:*

Los Angeles, California

*Interests and Organizations:*

Class of 2000 salutatorian from the University of California at Berkeley

B.A. Political Science

B.A. African-American studies (with honors)

> "The world is not dangerous because of those who do harm, but because of those who look at it without doing anything."

Enlightenment:
I believe that we all have an obligation to make the world a better place for our children and ourselves. The core reason that heinous crimes happen in the world is because some people stand by and allow them to. In different occurrences we are all empowered to take action against wrong. I am not saying that we are individual superheroes for every instance of wrongdoing we see, but we can make a difference. As black men, members of a race of people who have been barred from so many things throughout history, especially speaking out, we must be assertive, especially in our communities. This could be against any and all injustice or even when you see young brothers and sisters taking the wrong path in life.

## Therefore I Am
Age: 44
Occupation:
Pastor
City, State:
Miami, Florida
Interests and Organizations:
Defending those in need and aiding my fellow man.

> "Past the seeker as he prayed came the crippled, and the beggar, and the beaten. And seeing them, he cried, "Great God, how is it that a loving creator can see such things and yet do nothing about them?" God said, "I did do something. I made you."

Enlightenment:

There are many people suffering or living in degradation. We may ask ourselves why these things exist. We may further ask ourselves why these people are in these situations. This answer could come in a million and one forms from someone losing their job, to bad money management decisions, to any of a number of forms of addiction. I was once one of these people that others looked down on in society, a societal "pariah" if you will. I was homeless and slept in the streets on any bench or table I could call my bed for the night. It wasn't until someone reached out to me and said, "Brother, can I help you?" These words changed my life, both my physical situation of being homeless and the way I perceived the world. I now sit at my computer, in my apartment that I pay for. But I wouldn't be typing what this quote meant to me and how it changed my life if it wasn't for that brother who said, "Brother, can I help you?"

## Therefore I Am

*Age:* 46
*Occupation:*
Home Health Aide
*City, State:*
Louisville, Kentucky
*Interests and Organizations:*
Advocate for the homeless
Volunteer tutor for area homeless shelter

> ## "It is not only for what we do that we are held responsible, but also for what we do not do."

Enlightenment:

"Shut-Up!," a loud, baritone voice yelled through my paper-thin walls as I was eating my microwave meal. There was another voice, low but still very clear and it was that of a woman. It was the girlfriend of the owner of the baritone voice. This was not the first time I heard this, but I had recently seen the results of a night of yelling that echoed through my walls. I had seen her wear shades when it was raining outside. And nights after the yelling she would hurry past me the next day and barely speak, still wearing her shades so I could not get a good look at her.

Some things—you like to tell yourself—will work themselves out. Unfortunately, some things do not have the luxury of time to remedy them. So I decided I would be the remedy. I could no longer do nothing and continue to know the results of my doing nothing. I decided to go to the door. I knocked and was immediately attacked with a barrage of insults, and then things turned physical. Fortunately, the authorities showed up and the young lady pressed charges with prodding from the officers and me. This saying did not become my motto until after this incident, but I now apply it to all life's situations.

## Therefore I Am

*Age:* 41

*Occupation:*
Construction Site Manager

*City, State:*
Albany, New York

*Interests and Organizations:*
Football fanatic!

> ## "No man, not even the first, has made it anywhere without help from another man."

Enlightenment:

My uncle told this saying to me. He told me this to make me realize that no manor woman has made it to where they are without the help of others, so I should not fear accepting help to get from one point to another. It also taught me that no matter where you are in life, it is your responsibility to help pull others to where you are now. These words helped me to realize my responsibility as a black man and prompted me to begin to tutor, mentor, consult, and give of myself to the community at large. It has also taught me to recognize opportunities and grasp the hand waiting to pull me up. It is not as if I didn't do this before, but I now walk through life more consciously with one arm ahead of me and one behind me: one to grasp help and the opportunity created by it, and the other to pull my people with me.

### Therefore I Am

*Age:* 25

*Occupation:*

Analyst

*City, State:*

Brooklyn, New York

*Interests and Organizations:*

Member of Alpha Phi Alpha Fraternity, NAACP, Black Summit

> ## "No individual raindrop ever considers itself responsible for the flood."

Enlightenment:

Suppose you are walking down a busy street in your city or town. You have been chewing a piece of gum for most of the day. You are getting ready to go and get a bite to eat and you decide to toss the gum on the sidewalk. Now imagine if every person walking down this street is getting ready to toss his or her gum aside on the sidewalk. Eventually you will have a street that no one can walk down because of the masses of gum lining the pavement. You threw down one small piece of gum; you never thought that the walkway would end up like this. What many people say to themselves is that "I am only one person, I didn't really create this mess." But, *you did*! You may have well placed *all* the wads of gum in the street. You contributed to the outcome.

This quote has taught me to be responsible for all of my actions, no matter how small they may appear to me. We must remember that for every action there is an opposite reaction. We do not live life in a vacuum; what we do affects everything else.

### Therefore I Am

*Age:* 57

*Occupation:*
FBI

*City, State:*
Reno, Nevada

*Interests and Organizations:*
Rock climbing, trail biking, camping.
I am an avid outdoorsman/nature lover.

> ## "A child's life is like a piece of paper on which every person leaves a mark."

Enlightenment:
Why do I keep a clean home?
Because my mother kept our home spotless.
Why do I stay away from alcohol?
Because I never saw my father drink.
Why did I study hard and make the honor roll in school?
Because I saw my older brother do it.
Why do I say my prayers at night?
Because I heard my grandmother praying every night.

I make these points to show how impressionable we are as children and how still today children are influenced by what they hear and see. The world is not so different a place that we would have to totally change the way we were brought up. Though the days of sending letters to pen pals have been replaced by e-mails, and our Ataris have now succumbed to PlayStations and computer gaming, the same standards that we hold dear should still be instilled in our children. Don't let changing times change the impression you give to children.

## Therefore I Am
*Age:* 31
*Occupation:*
Foster Home Director
*City, State:*
Lansing, Michigan
*Interests and Organizations:*
Mentoring
Sunday school teaching
Playing bass in a band

# Point of View

## "Professionals built the Titanic; amateurs built the ark."

Enlightenment:

What makes a man? Is it the clothes he buys, the shoes on his feet, or the car that he drives? I find that we as a race of people with so many hindrances prejudices in society are often focused on the wrong things. We, at times, define ourselves through our material possessions. If a brother is seen driving a new Lexus he is in someway considered to be successful. Though we see him in his Lexus driving by seemingly with no worries, he is quietly wondering how he is going to pay his rent, electric bill, and gas because he just depleted his funds by paying his car payment.

Growing up, my siblings and I did not have the name brand jeans or the latest Air Jordan's. My parents taught us that clothes don't make the man, but the man makes the clothes. I never got better grades in school because I was wearing a Polo or Ralph Lauren shirt. I say all of this to reiterate what the quote means to me, just because it was done by "professionals" it does not necessarily mean it is the best.

## Therefore I Am

*Age:* 42

*Occupation:*

Chiropractor

*City, State:*

White Plains, New York

*Interests and Organizations:*

World traveling, foreign studies, foreign languages

---

## "When confronted with a Goliath-sized problem, which way do you respond: "He's too big to hit" or "He's too big to miss"?

Enlightenment:

I remember having to go to Bible school every summer when I was growing up. It would last anywhere from 3 to 4 weeks. I always enjoyed these summers, and even though I enjoyed it for the social aspects, I always did leave with a valuable lesson. Once in class, the teacher was going over the story of David and Goliath. This is the first time I heard, "When confronted with a Goliath-sized problem, which way do you respond: "He's too big to hit" or "He's too big to miss"?

At the time, I was sitting and engaging in conversation with my classmates, and the teacher called on me. After answering the question, we all got into a conversation talking about different situations or problems we have had in life and how we handled them. Along with the conversation among the class members, the quote gave me a totally new point of view for tackling life's problems.

---

## Therefore I Am

*Age:* 38

*Occupation:*

Children's Book Illustrator

*City, State:*

Houston, Texas

*Interests and Organizations:*

Computer art and design, free-hand drawing, painting

## "If all you have is a hammer, everything looks like the nail."

Enlightenment:

Multi-faceted. This is what we should all strive to be. To define *multi-faceted*, simply put, would be to have more than one skill or talent. Whenever you have one talent or skill, you will always be pigeonholed, or always placed in the same category as if not being able to do anything but your one skill or talent. This would be like having shackles on your hands and feet. My father worked at a tire company for 22 years. He worked 12-hour days Monday–Friday and 8-hour days on the weekend. After over two decades of working, giving his blood, sweat, and tears—the company closed. My father thought that after years of dedication to one company that whomever he would interview with would jump at the opportunity to hire such a faithful worker. However, this was not the case. He had everything from grocery stores to city trash pick-ups turn him down. What he thought was his greatest asset became his worst quality. He had only one approach, his dedication, with all of the jobs he would interview for, even though it worked with his previous company, the same "tool" cannot be used in all circumstances.

### Therefore I Am

*Age*: 22

*Occupation*:
Student, Taxi Cab Driver

*City, State*:
Washington, DC

*Interests and Organizations*:
Playing the trumpet in a band, jazz, blues, gospel (old school)

> **"There is always something to be thankful for. If you can't pay your bills, you can be thankful you are not one of your creditors."**

Enlightenment:

I was taught to say my prayers every night before I went to bed. I was taught to be thankful when I have a full stomach, and to be thankful when my stomach is empty.

You are always in a better situation than what you could be. There is a story of a little boy who would save all of his money to buy the coolest sneakers that the most popular celebrities would wear. All of his friends also had these shoes. The young boy would often complain to his mother that he hated his shoes and that everybody else had the popular shoes. His mother would reply to him, "You have shoes on your feet, so be thankful." But to no avail, the young boy was still set on getting his shoes. After a while, the boy had saved up enough money to get his shoes. On the way to the shoe store, his mother had to stop by the hospital to visit a friend. While at the hospital, the young boy saw several people in wheelchairs, not able to use their legs. He also saw patients that had amputations and did not have legs to use or feet to wear shoes. This is what it took to open the young boy's eyes. From that point on, he never complained.

I give this short excerpt and quote just to emphasize that we should always be thankful for the blessing that we have. We could always be in worse predicaments.

## Therefore I Am

*Age:* 37

*Occupation:*
Disc Jockey/Radio Personality

*City, State:*
Charlotte, North Carolina

*Interests and Organizations:*
Turntablist, Mixologist, Music Producer

## "It is the strong and silent waters that drown a man."

Enlightenment:

What may look like smooth sailing may not be. It is a common saying to choose a well-traveled path, the one with the smooth surfaces and paved roads. It is all too often that we get on these roads and expect nothing, and that is just when *something* happens. This is often how we are caught off guard and unprepared because we did not anticipate any problems. This is a weakness that I believe we as a race suffer from. We cannot depend on financial aid to go to school, have a back-up job. We cannot depend on the government for support in our later years—we cannot depend on Social Security, so invest now while you are working and strong. Don't wait for a problem to arise; take preventative measures whenever possible. You would never go into the desert without water because you know you would eventually get thirsty. Right?

Don't allow yourself to be fooled by the silent waters of life, be prepared in any and all situations, and always have a back-up plan.

### Therefore I Am
*Age:* 44
*Occupation:*
Nurse Practitioner
*City, State:*
Fond du Lac, Wisconsin
*Interests and Organizations:*
I head a nonprofit organization that dress as clowns to entertain at a pediatric facility. It's one of my life's love.

> ## "People do not quit playing because they grow old. They grow old because they quit playing."

Enlightenment:
In society, we are taught that numbers and age govern life. When we are 13 we are a teenager, when we are 16 we can get our driver's license, when we are 18 we can date who we want to date regardless of age, when we turn 21 we can buy alcohol, and in our sixties we can retire. Though we are constrained by certain statutes at certain ages, it should not change our spirit. Having these predetermined points of growth pulls us farther and farther away from who we truly are.

I learned this late in life. It was while visiting home after graduating from college and beginning to work that my mother said something to me that would change my life. She said, "Baby, how did you become older than your mother?" At the time, I did not understand, so I asked her what she meant. She replied, "Your spirit is old, I don't see my child in your eyes anymore. I don't see that young boy who liked to spend hours drawing or hours listening to music. When you stop playing son, you grow old. I should just go ahead and hand you my cane." It took a moment for this brief conversation to take hold of me. I could remember the exact times when I laid the things I enjoyed so much aside. It was at the stages in life at which society had deemed it time for me to change.

## Therefore I Am
*Age:* 41
*Occupation:*
Medical Software Developer
*City, State:*
Burlington, Vermont
*Interests and Organizations:*
Drawing and spending hours listening to music

## "Every road has two directions."

Enlightenment:

Papa would always tell us that the every road has two directions/destinations, and in life we are constantly at crossroads. There are points in time when we have to look both left and right to choose the correct path to take. Various circumstances come our way and we must make an informed decision. I have learned to weigh all of my options when making these decisions. I look at the good points and the not-so-good points of making a decision. My Papa taught us to ask these four questions when making decisions, or when we are at "the crossroads":

1.  What are the long-standing effects of the decision?
2.  Will it benefit me in the future or will it create a new problem?
3.  Did I look at all the options available to me?
4.  Is it a temporary fix to a current problem?

These questions have helped me become a better person and to have a prospering career, not to mention that it has kept me out of trouble. I hope they do the same for you.

## Therefore I Am

*Age:* 27

*Occupation:*
Air Force Pilot

*City, State:*
Olympia, Washington

*Interests and Organizations:*
Model airplanes, taking my family on educational excursions, spending romantic evenings with my wife

## "All sunshine makes the desert."

Enlightenment:

No one in this world can have a perfect day, week, month, or year. This is something that we must all realize. A lot of us pray, hope, and wish for everything to go well, and that we will have no problems. If we did not have problems, we would not even realize when something was good. We cannot grow without problems and challenges. These are the things that make us stronger.

For instance, let's just say that the sun always shined, this would make the world void of life. Without rain nothing grows. God has given us a perfect example of this right here in nature, in our faces everyday. You can just look at the world and how it renews itself and flourishes with rain and compare it to your life.

So when you have a problem, just work through it; this "rain" helps you grow, and the sun will be back.

### Therefore I Am
*Age:* 33
*Occupation:*
Electrical Powerline Installer
*City, State:*
Spartanburg, South Carolina
*Interests and Organizations:*
Participating in basketball, football, and baseball city leagues

## "Even in a pile of manure, a flower will grow."

Enlightenment:

Let me first start off by saying that I did not learn of the quote until I was an adult. It helped heal old wounds when I reflected back on my childhood. I lost my parents in an auto accident when I was about 8 years old. There were no family members that I could live with so I was placed in foster care. Now I am not in any way saying that all foster homes are bad, but the one that I lived in was horrible. Our caretaker would drink, and this would be the onset of her violent and abusive ways. At night, all the kids in the home would be battered and bruised, this night would constantly be repeated for years and years to come. The next day when she came to her senses she would fuss about the house being a mess, and the abuse would continue.

When I came of age, I did not internalize the horrible things that happened to me, nor did I use it as an excuse to do things that I was not supposed to be doing. I feel that many of us, as black men, rise up out of manure and we step in it almost on a daily basis. This shows our inner strength and determination. We must continue to grow and prosper.

### Therefore I Am

*Age:* 51

*Occupation:*
Political Spokesperson

*City, State:*
Sacramento, California

*Interests and Organizations:*
Eating right and staying healthy, both mentally and physically.
Pushing others to strive to be their best.

# Character

**"I have only one solution: To rise above this upsurge drama that others have staged around me."**

Enlightenment:

In my neighborhood there were drugs.

In my neighborhood there was violence.

In my neighborhood there was a short lifespan for young black men.

If you reached thirty in my neighborhood, you were considered a walking miracle.

This is where the above quote guided me in the right direction. There was no way I was going to follow in the footsteps of my friends, or so-called friends, and end up in a prison cell or a graveyard. All the bangin' & slangin' in the neighborhood would no way entangle me. At first, the fast money was very tempting—especially when I would see young guys my age driving expensive cars. Now, I can get whatever I need in a legitimate manner. Persistence and focus is the key: rise, brother, rise.

## Therefore I Am

*Age:* 30

*Occupation:*

Ph.D. student majoring in accounting, certified public account-ant

*City, State:*

Houston, Texas

*Interests and Organizations:*

Member of Alpha Phi Alpha Fraternity Inc.

## "Deeds of great men all remind us we should leave our past behind, but to leave positive steps, and, in parting, leave footprints in the sands of time."

Enlightenment:

All the actions that you take have repercussions. Where you have been and what you have done are part of the shadow that never leaves you. This is why it is of the utmost importance to watch whom you are with, where you are going, and the activities that you partake in. It is said that a man's good deeds far outshine his bad, but in the real world what do people bring up?

Personally, in my life, I have been a thief, vandal, and a hood. I have also been incarcerated 10 years of my life. Now, I am pursuing my PhD in business administration. I have recently been searching for a position using my master's degree to spearhead the effort but, my past always arises and acts as a roadblock. I am not saying that this is not at all fair, but it is a hindrance that keeps me from progressing in some instances. I have made my mistakes, and though I have totally turned my life around, my past comes back to haunt me. So be careful of all the decisions you make, they all have a tendency to have a boomerang effect.

### Therefore I Am

*Age:* 43
*Occupation:*
Customer Service Management
*City, State:*
Columbia, South Carolina
*Interests and Organizations:*
Hobbies include golf, badminton, basketball, and watching football; most of all, spending time with my sons.

## "Live so that you wouldn't be ashamed to sell the family parrot to the town gossip."

Enlightenment:
This is a family saying that has been passed down from generation to generation. It has kept my family at peace for a long time. One's home is a place of respect and understanding. There are usually no family squabbles, and we always keep our business within the realms of our own house. The family is the source of all strength and support; friends may come and go, but your family will always be your family.

### Therefore I Am
*Age:* 29
*Occupation:*
Physician Assistant
*City, State:*
Tulsa, Oklahoma
*Interests and Organizations:*
Big Brothers

> ## "One thing you can give, and still keep, is your word."

Enlightenment:

If you have nothing in life, you will always have your word. Though you may be lacking the material things in life, your word is more valuable than the crispest $100 dollar bill. I grew up in an impoverished and overpopulated government housing complex. None of us that lived there had anything. So in situations like these, all you have is your word. And once you "give" it and don't "keep" it, it is almost impossible to get it back (others' trust).

So when I gave someone my word that I would do something, I could always be trusted, because everyone knew me to be a person of my word.

## Therefore I Am
*Age:* 63
*Occupation:*
Restaurant Co-Owner
*City, State:*
Washington, DC
*Interests and Organizations:*
Community Activism

> "Be more concerned about your character than about your reputation, because your character is what you really are, while your reputation is merely what others think of you."

Enlightenment:

In several court cases, someone may be getting sued because of "defamation of character." Through this quote I learned that this "defamation of character" is not a real lawsuit. No one can change who you truly are. They can attempt to change your reputation, and unfortunately they may even be successful. But *you* are the only person who can change your character. Do not let other persons, places, things, or situations change you without your knowing and, even more importantly, your permission. Stand strong.

## Therefore I Am
*Age*: 59
*Occupation*:
Professor
*City, State*:
St. Louis, Missouri
*Interests and Organizations*:
Father, grandfather, all-around family man

> "The ultimate measure of a man is not where he stands in moments of comfort and convenience, but where he stands at times of challenge and controversy."

Enlightenment:
It is easy to stand up and voice your opinion when everything is going your way or when, in the presence of others, everybody shares your same view. Maturation and growth come in times of conflict, and it is at this point that we grow and remold ourselves. Facing various challenges and controversies are stepping stones for a man's character, ideals, and beliefs. What he gains for himself is more self-esteem and confidence, while, in the eyes of his peers, he gains respect and sometimes notoriety. One should always stand up and let his opinions or views be known.

## Therefore I Am
*Age:* 26
*Occupation:*
Telecommunications Management
*City, State:*
Roanoke, Virginia
*Interests and Organizations:*
Concerned Black Men, Inc.

## "I will permit no man to narrow and degrade my soul by making me hate him."

<u>Enlightenment:</u>

In my life, I have come across people who did not like me for who I am or did not like me because of the things that I stood for or believed in. I would often see little things that they would do when they thought I was not looking or heard things "hearsay" from a third party. I was raised not to degrade or tarnish myself just to show my malice or disdain for someone else. This will only make the situation worse and cause things to escalate.

One thing that I learned in these situations is to meet hate with love. Whenever I would be in one of these situations, I would be pleasant around the person and greet and speak to him or her like they were one of my best friends. I've come to realize in the face of love and kinship, hatred will make an about-face.

### <u>Therefore I Am</u>
<u>Age:</u> 42
<u>Occupation:</u>
Banking and Commercial Loan Processing Manager
<u>City, State:</u>
Atlanta, Georgia
<u>Interests and Organizations:</u>
100 Black Men of America, NAACP

"How far you go in life depends on your being tender with the young, compassionate with the aged, sympathetic with the striving, and tolerant of the weak and the strong—because some day in life you will have been all of these."

Enlightenment:

There are many stages that we go through in our lives, and the above quote captures each one. You will one day look through the eyes of youth, old age, times when you are striving, and times of being weak and strong. These are also the states that you will see communities in. We were not put here to push aside the weak, hate the strong, disrespect our elders, misguide our youth, or hinder the striving. One should imagine being in their shoes because one day you will be.

How would you like the world to treat you at these points in life? Your answer to this question should now be your actions.

### Therefore I Am

*Age:* 29

*Occupation:*
Sales Promotion Manager

*City, State:*
Little Rock, Arkansas

*Interests and Organizations:*
Hip-hop and Urban music, any and all types of sports;
Member of Association of African American Role Models

# Diligence

## "All the so-called "secrets of success" will not work unless you do."

Enlightenment:

Almost everyone that you meet has a secret to success. Some of these people may be speaking from experience and some from what they heard or read from some self-help guru's writings. Whatever the case, you can have every path, opportunity, and "secret" to success imaginable, but success will not fall out of the sky into your lap. The game of life gives you what you give it. The most successful people did not become successful by chance. They were not sitting around and success did not simply drop into their lap. It took hard work, focus, and, most importantly, dedication. When I set my sights on my career, my eyes did not wander from my goal. I worked diligently in school and internships to get the recognition and position that I thought I deserved.

### Therefore I Am
Age: 36
Occupation:
Rehabilitation Department Manager
City, State:
Charlotte, North Carolina
Interests and Organizations:
Antique collecting, rebuilding classic cars

## "An obstacle is something you see when you take your eyes off the goal."

Enlightenment:
Money and time are the two things that I have heard throughout my life that have been major obstacles to others. I have even heard its being used for an excuse. When you have your eyes set on the goal, these and other things will not stand in your way.

I say this from my own personal experience. I successfully completed medical school while holding a part-time job in the morning before classes and a full time job afterward, all while maintaining my grades. I am not saying this to brag or boast, but to let you know that all things are possible. There is no person, place, or thing that can hold you back when you are determined to reach your goal. Jump over every hurdle that you come to in life all while looking at the finish line.

## Therefore I Am
*Age:* 37
*Occupation:*
Physician (Geriatrics)
*City, State:*
Washington, DC
*Interests and Organizations:*
Howard University Alumni, business owner and entrepreneur

> ## "Don't be afraid of opposition; remember that a kite rises against, not with the wind."

Enlightenment:

My Mother has always told me, "Don't be afraid of opposition; remember that a kite rises against, not with the wind." When I was younger, I never really understood the saying. I just thought she was saying it because we were not at all wealthy or even well to do. We went through so many hardships when it came to making ends meet.

My father passed when I was 12 and my mother had to raise four girls and two boys all on her own. I believe this is the point where I would hear the expression on almost a daily basis. My mother would tell my brother and sisters and me to meet all of our challenges head on and it would make us better persons, stronger persons. Doing this, like the kite, you will rise over your adversities and soar.

## Therefore I Am
*Age:* 44
*Occupation:*
Guidance Counselor
*City, State:*
Gallagher, MA
*Interests and Organizations:*
PlayStation fanatic, Male Mentoring Program of Gallagher

## "Don't wait for your ship to come in, row out to meet it."

Enlightenment:
Do any of the following sound familiar to you?

"I'll be straight when my income tax comes in," or "I'll be glad when things change around here (neighborhood conditions, police brutality, etc)."

These are things that I have heard throughout the African-American community for so long. Though some of us have tried to make a difference, many of us remain stagnant. A lot of people seem to believe that if you wait long enough, what you want will happen or come to pass. Brothers, this is not true! If there is something that you want changed or circumstances that you want altered, you have to take the initiative to do things yourself.

### Therefore I Am
*Age:* 31
*Occupation:*
Docking Technician
*City, State:*
Staten Island, New York
*Interests and Organizations:*
Sailing, Racing boats

---

## "It is not the size of the dog in the fight, but the size of the fight in the dog."

---

Enlightenment:

One of my most powerful assets is that I am often underestimated. Now you may be thinking, how is being underestimated an asset? Well listen carefully and this maybe an asset you can harness for yourself. First, the underestimation comes in the simple form of who I am. A black man. When others see me, they see what the television shows, news broadcasts, and music videos show them of people that look like me. They think either that I am going to try to rob them, I am going to start to rap, I am on my way to a basketball court, or I am about to say or do something ignorant. Here lies my "advantage." My outside appearance allows me to place myself in advantageous and strategic positions because I do not seem like a "threat." When I say *threat*, I am not referring to a danger or a hazard, but rather the threat of breaking the shackles of the image that society has so deemed to lay upon me. It is not what is on the outside that guides you and gives you drive, but what you hold in your heart, mind, and soul that will determine your place in life.

---

### Therefore I Am
*Age:* 29
*Occupation:*
Graduate Student
*City, State:*
Yonkers, New York
*Interests and Organizations:*
Independent film directing, Campus Investment Group member

> ## "Tears will get you sympathy.
> ## Sweat will get you results."

Enlightenment:
Stop complaining and feeling sorry for yourself. You are wasting valuable time that you can never get back.

Some may think this is harsh, but sometimes the truth is harsh and hard to deal with. The world knows that we were enslaved and about all the injustices that we suffered as a people. Our ancestors have endured this maltreatment and torture, and that is why we are here today. My forefathers would not want me standing around complaining about how "The Man" is holding me down in an unjust system and that racism is prevalent every-where. *We all know this!*

Though we must not forget these things, we at times need to look forward and work harder toward our aspirations without "cry-ing" and making excuses. Just as our ancestors worked hard in the so-called masters' fields, we still have the same capacity to persevere and achieve what we wish. You get out of life what you put into it.

### Therefore I Am
*Age:* 33
*Occupation:*
Software Developer
*City, State:*
Baltimore, Maryland
*Interests and Organizations:*
Collecting electronic gizmos, going to church every Sunday morning with my family (wife, two boys, one girl), and being a good example for my children

> ## "The person who moves a mountain starts by carrying away small stones."

Enlightenment:

What I learned from this saying is that nothing happens overnight—whether you want to be the CEO of your own company, walk on Mars, or become anything in the world. You must first have a beginning. It is far from realistic that you will just be hired or discovered at random. Anything worth having is something that you have to labor hard for. To be on this path takes patience and diligence; in the end, you will discover that you can actually move mountains and look back at what you achieved with a sense of pride and dignity.

## Therefore I Am

Age: 20

Occupation:

Student

City, State:

Passaic, New Jersey

Interests and Organizations:

Website development, Homeless shelter volunteer

## "A man is not finished when he is defeated. He is finished when he quits."

Enlightenment:

Defeat is not the end of it all, and I speak from personal experience. I feel that I have been defeated on several occasions but I have yet to give in to this defeat and stop trying to achieve. I began college and successfully got through my first year with an excellent GPA. I was on top of the world. This high didn't last for long; in the next semester, my financial aid was stopped. I tried desperately to find a solution, but to no avail. I met with defeat.

There was no way I was going to stand for this. I had to keep pushing on, I was adamant about getting a college education. With this in mind, I worked retail, I tutored, I mowed lawns, and even worked as a janitor the semester that I was off. By the time the next semester rolled around I had earned enough to pay for the next two semesters and, lo and behold, I got a full scholarship. Now, if I would have stopped and bowed down to defeat, I would not have made any progress at all.

### Therefore I Am
*Age:* 57
*Occupation:*
Banking Executive
*City, State:*
Fort Myers, Florida
*Interests and Organizations:*
Investment banking, Online stock trading

**"Though no one can go back and make a brand-new start, anyone can start from now and make a brand-new beginning."**

Enlightenment:

We have all made mistakes that we wish we could erase. This mistake could have changed your life totally. It could be dropping out of school, fathering a child out of wedlock, hustling, or a number of other things that you wish you could undo.

I write this to tell you that there is hope. There is no need to let your past mentally enslave you. Holding on to these negativities can only make you feel worthless, hopeless, and have no self-respect. This can often lead back to the same trenches that you so despise. You have the power within yourself to begin again, to sow a new garden of hope and prosperity from this point on.

I write to you as a successful entrepreneur and *former* felon.

Always keep your head up.

## Therefore I Am
*Age:* 35
*Occupation:*
Author/Motivational speaker
*City, State:*
Dyersburg, Tennessee
*Interests and Organizations:*
Opening caged minds to their full potential

# "He who wants the rose must first respect the thorn."

Enlightenment:

In our front yard when I was growing up, my grandfather had a rose bush. He would tell me to go and pick a rose, put it in a vase, and give one to my mother and one to my grandmother. I can't begin to tell you how many pricks I received from the rose bush trying to complete my grandfather's requested task.

After almost tears came to my eyes and little dots of blood filled my fingers and palms of my hands he called me over to the porch. He then told me, as I looked up at him with glassy eyes, "he who wants the rose must respect the thorn." He explained to me that the most beautiful and wanted things have obstacles that you must learn to overcome in order to attain them. This quote taught me the value of ingenuity, patience, and assiduousness, and I continue to find it invaluable today.

## Therefore I Am

*Age:* 43

*Occupation:*

Agriculture/Farmer

*City, State:*

Gulfport, Mississippi

*Interests and Organizations:*

Member of church choir, organist, Sunday school teacher

# Relationships

> ## "The desire of love is to give. The desire of lust is to get."

Enlightenment:

I have been in many relationships for many different reasons. Some were just for simple friendship, some companionship, and some even just to have a physical relationship. Whatever the case may be, it is wise to be honest with yourself, and with the person whom you have the relationship with, about your intentions. A good method my mother used to tell me, when evaluating a relationship, is to ask myself if I want to give, get, or give and get in this relationship.

Being honest with yourself and your companion once you know the answer to this question can save a lot of potentially wasted time and energy or can truly blossom into something wonderful.

## Therefore I Am

_Age:_ 29

_Occupation:_
Convention and Meeting Manager

_City, State:_
Brooklyn, New York

_Interests and Organizations:_
Social and Political Organizations
Concerned Black Men—National Chapter

## "One of the most important things a father can do for his children is to love their mother."

Enlightenment:

I've seen women beaten and bruised and later in tons of makeup trying to hide what their boyfriend or husband did to them at home. It is sad to think that children may have been witness to this. This is what they learn or perceive to be normal. It is also a push in the wrong direction in the view of women.

I have also seen mommies and daddies holding hands in the park. A child becomes whatever he or she sees (especially a little boy). The quote above is what every father should be doing. This teaches the respect that we at times lack in our society of radios constantly blaring "bitches" and "hos."

## Therefore I Am

*Age:* 33

*Occupation:*

Social Worker/Child Advocate

*City, State:*

Detroit, Michigan

*Interests and Organizations:*

Hip-hop teaching and preaching. Reaching youth through hip-hop.

> "To say that a man cannot love one woman at a time is ridiculous. It is like saying a musician needs more than one violin to play the same piece of music."

Enlightenment:

If there was ever a man to cut out on his wife, it had to be my father. At first, it was subtle and he made excuses for coming in late. Eventually it got to a point where he would stay away from home for three to four days and not even call or offer an explanation. I could never understand why a man, when he has something good in his life, a beautiful wife, and children who adored him would want to risk and lose it all for another woman with whom he has only physical ties. But if you still have these urges and are planning to get married—*don't*. When you find that special woman, remember: you only need one.

## Therefore I Am
*Age:* 31
*Occupation:*
Professor of English
*City, State:*
Chapel Hill, North Carolina
*Interests and Organizations:*
Board of Education Advisor, Currently writing a novel

> ## "An ounce of regret never made an a bit of difference."

Enlightenment:
What is done cannot be undone. Our words give us the power to change the world. There have been great orators throughout our race that have inspired us to be our best and realize that, "I am somebody." Not only does the power of speech invoke empowerment, but it can also result in degradation of the soul. When someone cuts you, physically, the wound will heal. If someone hurts your feelings or insults you, it takes longer for the pain to go away—if it ever does. This quote led me to realize that words once spoken cannot be retracted, that there are no band-aids for a wounded self-esteem except for time, and that in itself sometimes will not be the remedy. Saying that you're sorry or regret your actions is not going to change a thing, so be forewarned about the power of your mouth: choose what you say to others with caution.

*Especially what you say to the sisters*: A woman's memory is much more longstanding than a man's.

### Therefore I Am
*Age*: 24
*Occupation*:
Computer Information System Administrating Manager
*City, State*:
Houston, Texas
*Interests and Organizations*:
Healthcare Advocate for Minorities, Volunteer for Welfare-to-Work program, Meals-on-Wheels driver

"Creation of a woman was from the rib of man:
She was not made from his head to top him;
nor out of his feet to be trampled upon by him;
But out of his side to be equal with him,
under his arm to be protected,
And near his heart to be loved."

Enlightenment:
I first heard this quote in a sermon at church. Not only was it awakening for me, but also it was interesting to see and hear the congregation's reaction. In most churches, you become acquainted with other families, whether it's just in church or in the community as well. So you get to know about their family life, goals, aspirations, and their outlooks on life. When I was noticing my fellow church members' reactions to this statement, it seemed obvious what went on in other houses. The men and women that had good relationships and that agreed with the pastor smiled, nodded, and embraced one another or held hands. The men that didn't necessarily degree remained emotionless with no reaction at all, just a blank stare toward the pulpit where the speaker was standing, whereas wives or companions just looked toward them with a sort of smirk.

Your duty as a man is to love, respect, and care for your woman. She should not be above or below you, but right by your side.

## Therefore I Am
*Age:* 26
*Occupation:*
Hotel Reservation Supervisor
*City, State:*
Jackson, Tennessee
*Interests and Organizations:*
Phi Beta Sigma Fraternity, NAACP

## "The best way to overcome temptation is to avoid the tempting situation."

Enlightenment:

My father told me this when I was first married. We sat and spoke about how life was going to change for me. He spoke of my friends (the single ones) coming over and asking me to hang out with them in the same spots we always have and that they may expect me to be the same person. Whenever we would go out, most of the time, we would try to meet women. Being in an environment where there are several beautiful women, revealingly clothed, and in a party, "I'm enjoying life" atmosphere, is a tempting situation. We also spoke of other situations that may turn out to be "tempting." This included everything from drinking irresponsibly to communicating with old girlfriends. I didn't believe everything that he said, and I thought some of the things he talked about were a little extreme, but I understood perfectly what he was trying to relay to me. I liken it to putting a compulsive gambler in Las Vegas or Atlantic City with $10,000 dollars in his pocket. This is his tempting situation; the possibility of his indulgence in gambling would be less likely to occur if he were not in this environment.

### Therefore I Am

*Age:* 34

*Occupation:*

Machine Tool Cutting Operator

*City, State:*

Asbury Park, New Jersey

*Interests and Organizations:*

The Association of Community Organizations
for Reform Now (ACORN),

Single African American Father Exchange member

# Prosperity

### "A goal properly set is halfway reached."

<u>Enlightenment</u>:

Having a vision of where you want to be is the key to getting there. A lot of young brothers say that they are going to do this or that but never actually reach their goal. This is because the goal was not properly set. One has to realize that you just can't say that you are going to do something or accomplish a task; you have to take the "steps" to get there. Those who are where they want to be set the goals as well as make sacrifices to complete their goals.

### Therefore I Am

<u>Age</u>: 44

<u>Occupation</u>:

Restaurant Manager

<u>City, State</u>:

Yonkers, New York

<u>Interests and Organizations</u>:

Computers, Japanese animation, and cooking

---

## "Ask yourself if what you are doing today is getting you closer to where you want to be tomorrow."

Enlightenment:
What do you want in life? Is standing on the corner chillin,' or being at that club until 3 o'clock in the morning getting you to where you want to be? Or is it that the time spent in the club could have been better utilized writing up that business plan or working on that new idea you had. My father always stressed the importance of time management to me. He would often tell my brothers and me that for every second you spend doing nothing, your competition is gaining ground.

---

### Therefore I Am
*Age:* 34
*Occupation:*
Orthopedic Surgeon
*City, State:*
Concord, Massachusetts
*Interests and Organizations:*
Mentoring—exposing our youth to things that they would not encounter on an everyday basis.

> ## "Destiny is not a matter of chance, it is a matter of choice; it is not a thing to be waited for, it is a thing to be achieved."

Enlightenment:

Get off your butt and do what you have to do. You have probably heard in movies, "It is your destiny," being said to the main character, meaning that, whatever you do, the same result will occur. Wake up, my friend; we are not in the movies. In this world, you have to work for what you want. Your destiny is not going to miraculously be fulfilled while you do nothing. My family taught me that I have to take the initiative to do what I want to do to achieve the things that I want to achieve. I've also learned, with my family's guidance, that with my determination and tenacity, anything is possible.

## Therefore I Am

*Age:* 25

*Occupation:*

Comedian/Cartoonist

*City, State:*

Los Angeles, California

*Interests and Organizations:*

Giving our community laughs,

Spending time with my daughters

NAACP member, drawing and art

# "Don't limit your challenges; challenge your limits."

Enlightenment:

It was several years ago that my Psychology 101 professor enlightened me with this statement. He first spoke of this when we were discussing the fight-or-flight response. Following the lecture, he closed the class with this quote. After class, I spoke to him about the quote and he said that some of us limit ourselves because we avoid adversity and challenges. He went on to say that challenges enable us to survive, adapt, and become better. He gave the example that we would have remained "cavemen" if we didn't have the challenges of catching, fighting, and hunting creatures that are bigger, stronger, and faster than we are. We had the challenge of out-thinking these animals—our survival depended on it.

Today we should maintain the mentality that we have challenges (in all shapes and forms) and should face them as though our very existence depended on it. In today's times we are not only the hunters, but also the hunted.

## Therefore I Am

*Age:* 59

*Occupation:*
Psychologist/University Professor

*City, State:*
Washington, DC

*Interests and Organizations:*
Teaching and guiding the minds of tomorrow. Human rights advocacy. Vietnam veteran.

---

## "It is not how busy you are, but why you are busy— the bee is praised, the mosquito is swatted."

Enlightenment:

How wisely do you spend your time? I ask this because when I call friends up, sometimes they say that they are busy. I often ask myself, busy doing what? I ask myself this, not because I'm nosey, but because of the saying my grandfather would say to us. He would emphasize using your time wisely. He would say that there are two types of people, those who are like bees and those who are like mosquitoes. Those who are like bees are focused and stay on task because they have a goal in mind. Those who are like mosquitoes buzz around like bees but don't have a real purpose.

He would always call all of the grandkids his little worker bees and would describe us this way at all family functions. This quote kept me focused all through college, a time when you have to be a bee to stay on top of things.

---

## Therefore I Am
Age: 44
Occupation:
Aircraft Maintenance Mechanic
City, State:
Honolulu, Hawaii
Interests and Organizations:
Flying my plane
Collecting model planes and model ships

## "Plan ahead: it wasn't raining when Noah built the ark."

Enlightenment:

It pays to plan ahead for any circumstance that you can foresee. Imagine right now that you get a call on the phone and the company you work for tells you that your services are no longer required. This is the exact thing that happened to my father.

When he received this call, he remained calm and called my mother into their bedroom. He told her, and my brother and I knew something was wrong because we heard her start to cry. My father then called my brother and me and told us that things might be changing some. Following his breaking the news to us, he took us to the girl's room. Here he said to us, "Boys, in life things happen. You can never be prepared for everything, but you can be prepared for some." Then he said this quote, "Plan ahead, it wasn't raining when Noah built the ark." He then proceeded to lift the mattress of my sister's crib and showed us a small stash of money. That stash of money carried us for two months until my father got a new job. So this is a lesson that has stuck with me and will be instilled in my children.

### Therefore I Am

*Age:* 39

*Occupation:*
E-Commerce Manager

*City, State:*
Akron, Ohio

*Interests and Organizations:*
Web designing, Homeless shelter volunteer

## "Dwell not upon thy weariness; thy strength shall be according to the measure of thy desire."

Enlightenment:

I am the preacher's son. So I grew up hearing about every bible verse, quote, and saying in the bible. Whenever I would misbehave I would be hit with a bible verse. The time that a verse stayed in my mind was actually when I was about 17. There were several things going on in my life. I was preparing for the SAT, I was a student athlete, and I had to maintain my grades and earn no less than a B. I would complain about how much I had to do and get a little depressed. It was then that my mother, not my sermon-giving father said, "Dwell not upon thy weariness; thy strength shall be according to the measure of thy desire." And it sunk in. The more I want, and the more my desire, the more energy I would have to put toward that goal. I now apply this quote to everything in life. To whatever I want to accomplish, I say this in the back of my mind. When I talk to my parents now that I am a grown man, I often remind my mother of those influential words.

### Therefore I Am
*Age*: 28
*Occupation*:
CAD Drafter
*City, State*:
Greenbrier, Tennessee
*Interests and Organizations*:
Computer Gaming
Assistant Professor/Lecturer

## "If you ever need a helping hand, there is one at the end of your arm."

Enlightenment:

I have always been taught that God helps those who help themselves. All too often, some of us ask for help without attempting to remedy the problem ourselves. In my opinion, and some may disagree, we are the first people with our hand out, be it arguing about reparations or to receive government-allocated monies (welfare, etc.). These programs are necessary for some of us but at times these services are abused.

I am from the school of thought that a man does what he has to do to provide for his family. There is a certain pride in being able to put food on your family's table. So I say to you when you are in need of a helping hand, try to help yourself first.

### Therefore I Am
*Age:* 54
*Occupation:*
Chief Loan Officer
*City, State:*
Portland, Oregon
*Interests and Organizations:*
Rebuilding & remodeling homes
Online Investing

> **"If a bird is flying for pleasure, it flies with the wind, but if it meets danger it turns and faces the wind, in order that it may rise higher."**

Enlightenment:
My mother is Black and my father is Native American. I have withstood a million and one different racist ideas and comments. And my quote has helped me deal with my life. Initially, when I would hear comments I would not face them and would turn away. It wasn't until my mother said this quote to me that I was able to stand up for myself.

It is sad to say, however, that I have heard racist remarks even from African-Americans, which *I consider myself to be*. I tell those African-Americans who made those racist comments that when a racist person of another race/culture sees me, they don't see me as a mixed person. They see me as a nigger with long hair. So I leave this quote to let every man know to face his adversity. Let us not be divided; our diversity is what makes us strong. Continue to rise.

## Therefore I Am
*Age:* 28
*Occupation:*
Administrative Assistant
*City, State:*
Wilmington, North Carolina
*Interests and Organizations:*
Researching my ancestry
Teaching children on the Navajo reservation
Weight training & body building

# Hope

## "God creates a worm for every bird, but he does not throw it in the nest."

Enlightenment:
What is it that you want? Have you been searching for that thing for what seems like an eternity? You are not alone. There are several people that feel this way. Know that the thing that you are searching for is out there.

My insight comes from looking for love and trying to find that significant other. Though I learned this saying a long time ago, I always kept it close to heart to give myself hope. At times I grew weary and wanted to give up but I kept my eyes and ears open. When I first heard my wife's voice, I knew that I was going to marry her. Now the quote, which I learned so long ago, is being passed down to my son.

### Therefore I Am
*Age:* 41
*Occupation:*
Social Worker
*City, State:*
Detroit, Michigan
*Interests and Organizations:*
Men of Color Motivational Group, Black Men for the Eradication of Sexism

## "It is the wounded oyster that mends itself with a pearl."

Enlightenment:

In our deepest times of sorrow and despair, we can be our own worst enemy or our own best friend. In times when we are down, if we keep our heads to the sky and not at the ground we can move forward. Throughout African-American history we can see how adversity has caused a people to strive and change the world as they new it. Take this strength from your ancestors—it is within you when you have hit what you have perceived to be rock bottom—realize this: There is nowhere to go but up.

### Therefore I Am
*Age:* 59
*Occupation:*
Employee Benefit Account Manager
*City, State:*
Columbus, Ohio
*Interests and Organizations:*
Association of African American Role Models

## "Vision is not seeing things as they are, but as they will be."

Enlightenment:

I am poor, broke, and lonely. Currently I am a college student. I didn't come from a wealthy or even middle class family, so I have to work to put myself through school. I am in my last year of medical school and I am completing my residency at a local hospital in the day and I work a full time job in the evening and on the weekends. This limits me from having any real social life, and since I have to pay for things like tuition, lab fees, and expensive textbooks for class, I'm left broke with barely enough to pay rent and buy food. But finally, I see the light at the end of the tunnel; I am almost there. The quote above has helped me stay focused; it has helped me to keep my eyes on the prize. It has helped me not to get sidetracked by clubs and bad relationships, which I believe to sometimes be a deterrent to brothers' reaching the status that they are capable of. I may have missed a few parties, but in the end it is worth it. In life you have to have foresight or you will always be blindsided by situations.

### Therefore I Am

*Age:* 23

*Occupation:*
Student, Medical University of South Carolina

*City, State:*
Charleston, South Carolina

*Interests and Organizations:*
Biking, hiking, tennis

> "You must not lose faith in humanity. Humanity is an ocean, if a few drops of the ocean are dirty, the ocean does not become dirty."

Enlightenment:
When we watch the news, it is seldom that the camera is focused on the Black man who is working on his second PhD, or the Black man functioning as a single parent raising two daughters, or the Black man working to better his community. What is typically presented on the evening news is African-American neighborhood violence, talk of a multimillion-dollar hip-hop star and his misdeeds, or the all time classic—a black man being put in handcuffs.

Not only are the images portrayed affecting other races' views of African-American males, but it is slowly creeping into the African-American community as well. This is the type of thinking that can erode a society from within. Just because these problems exist in our society, we are not all involved in negativity. So the next time you see a negative news story or someone makes a stereotypical comment on black men and negativity, just remember this quote and pass the quote along.

## Therefore I Am

*Age:* 29
*Occupation:*
Mechanical Engineering Manager
*City, State:*
South Bend, Indiana
*Interests and Organizations:*
100 Black Men of America

> ## "*Always* and *never* are two words to always remember never to use."

Enlightenment:
There are no absolutes in life, except death. No one can tell you that you are unable to achieve your hopes, dreams, and aspirations. Whenever you are trying to accomplish something, there will always be that person there who will tell you that you can't do it. Just smile, and prove them wrong.

### Therefore I Am
*Age:* 33
*Occupation:*
National Sales Manager
*City, State:*
Orange County, California
*Interests and Organizations:*
A proud member of America's armed forces; Air Force

## "Courage is when fear says a prayer."

Enlightenment:

This saying gives me great hope in my time of despair. I feel that when fear is in control nothing can be accomplished, so to say a prayer before you do anything gives you the courage and the will to succeed.

### Therefore I Am

Age: 23

Occupation:

Student

City, State:

Washington, District of Columbia

Interests and Organizations:

Graduate Student at the Maryland Eastern Shore

Alpha Phi Alpha Fraternity

> ## "There are only two things in life: blessings and blessings in disguise."

Enlightenment:
I created the above saying to remind my loved ones and myself that there is always a blessing, even in the most horrific circumstances. It is up to each of us to discover what that blessing is, assuming we can muster the strength to look for it.

### Therefore I Am
*Age:* 47
*Occupation:*
Astrologer
*City, State:*
Palm Desert, California
*Interests and Organizations:*
Political Activism

> ## "There is nothing in a caterpillar that tells you it's going to be a butterfly.

Enlightenment:
Look at yourself and tell me what you see. Do you see what you were, what you are, or what you are going/striving to be? This question is extremely important. If you just see your past or what you were, you may be looking back at all the mistakes that you have made and allowing them to weigh you down—instead of moving forward. If you see only who you are now, you are lacking foresight and will be unable to maneuver yourself now for what you want later. And if you see only what you are trying to be, you may be rushing while trying to attain the goal but not thinking of all of your options available for attaining that goal. To be a success, you need to be able to see all views.

Others may see you as just some guy walking down the street. But only you know what is inside, and only you can release your full potential.

### Therefore I Am
Age: 37
*Occupation:*
Cellular and Paging Distributor
*City, State:*
Maitland, Florida
*Interests and Organizations:*
Sigma Phi Rho Fraternity, Inc.

# *Author's Thoughts*

I hope that these ideas and words have not only inspired you, but will also keep you focused and motivated despite any obstacle that may lie in your path. We come from a long history of people who have succeeded against insurmountable odds. Your path lies before you. All of your goals and aspirations are achievable if you remain task oriented and goal focused.

Writing this book and receiving thousands of replies from men who look like me and have the same interests and concerns that I do was an inspiration in itself. It showed me that we are still in the struggle despite what the media may say. We have the power to change our neighborhoods, communities, cities, and even a nation. We have succeeded in the past, and our future will be no different.

Stay strong in the struggle,
Frederick B. Covington

0-595-34283-3

www.ingramcontent.com/pod-product-compliance
Lightning Source LLC
Chambersburg PA
CBHW031300280526
45784CB00004B/1921